We're Going to Need a Higher Fence

We're Going to Need a Higher Fence

Jennifer MacBain-Stephens

Lit
Fest
Press

ISBN: 978-1-943170-29-6

Cover Art: Susan Yount

Interior and Cover Design: Jane L. Carman

Published by Lit Fest Press, Carman, 688 Knox Road 900 North,
Gilson, Illinois 61436

Lit Fest Press

Outside the box

Contents

Bird Poem #1

poorly illustrated legs/ no passion filled gallop/ lacking blood lust / ingest weight, repeat /dreaming of index fingers / acquiesce: a torso/ bird brain glass smash/ no forehead to inspect/ no fingertips to soothe / cat egos placate / survival of the fastest/ fly away feathers/ flutter in the bath/ pretend it's a game / I can shoot you full of buckshot /no safe house too small.

The Hour

The hour refuses to pose for the camera.
The hour was drenched by a Garland of Roses.

The hour was prepping to stud.
The jockey sits with his legs crossed,

drinks a cup of tea. The tea
grows cold too quickly.

(It whinnies at this, the hour.)
The hour is in the stable

with a stop watch
strapped to its back,

prepping for the most exciting two minutes in sports.
It is really the best place for the hour,

it doesn't have personal belongings.
Keeping up with the cleaning

was the end of the hour.
All the suitors are women.

They have the lightest caresses the
hour ever felt. The hour

barely feels its second hand.
The hour nibbles an apple core

from each gloved palm.
This makes the hour's day.

The hour is a stallion at day,
a colt by night.

Sometimes a sun dial or a goat stirs up drama.
The hour couldn't ask for a better
time honored tradition really.

It's the memories, though, that get
to the hour.
It can't make them fast enough.

statoblast

masses of cells that function as "survival pods"

I obsessively count tentacles.

The sunburst feelers at the end – colicky muppet hair

Adorable in its minuteness

if it wasn't attached to the parent colony

Your globule prism escape podded into my time out.

Carried along on animals or floating vegetation,

like a shoplifter who stole my favorite lip gloss

you stole my heart.

Blast me to the core,

hang onto my divided cells,

survive freezing and desiccation

I cannot cuddle you in diseased waters

A secret sedan lover-

why are humans afraid

of multiple, flailing limbs?

Long fingers taste, grope.

We are accustomed to the language of the torso.

A gooey center is the best part

in molten chocolate cake

There is a center, a sun.

Veins are excruciating.

To see them lying in the road

or on the slab

or inside something's something.

I gather you under the microscope

push you away from where you want to go.

A frog toe shaped algae waterbed.

Blind little bat.

Like Lear, you stumbled when you saw.

valve

My xx balks at algebraic equations.
Variable "*n*" chooses storm shelter
over internet connection.
Big brains shut up in a shed.

We all went missing in university
basements. It is awful,
I know, until it isn't
memories imprisoned in a jam jar.

Formaldehyde hose humble pies itself,
twists into No Access Pass chromosomes.
Involuntary walking like a throat
changing its mind,
hearing verses listening.

An open and shut barbed wire
purse mobilizes,
wants to see how it feels
on the outside,

shuns its velvety walls.
Fluidize solids,
or slurries,
seal a choice switch blade.

Open a mechanical greeting card.
Thieve my face, now
on a bumper sticker
even low pressure systems knew

I was lost and found on a milk carton.
The fridge door swings open-
poorly installed.

Bird Poem #2

Icterus Baltimore Aquus Marinus
For the artist (unknown) outside the Museum of Found American Art

Cement invaded a tiny mold
beak, wings, feet.
mirrored glass pieces
encased refraction forever
or the weather wins

A Technicolor environmentalist's
vision in sharp shards.

In your torso, my eyes radiate chartreuse
My chin lavender,
My parka disintegrates into
diamond suns.

Now I have wings

I soar into pieces
The dirt, formidable
The ice, suffocating

No longer encased in stone
swallow the wind.

gold sunshine purity mix

seed pods float across landfills
like impulsive sexts

a deadhead surfaces, once , twice,
sinks under dandelion hordes

the throne drowns under seaweed
the struggle to coerce

petals is female,
like polka dot design

refer to missed cheek kisses
like a fact checking error

sample a midnight special
fun size it,

sheets of plastic cover the floor

Saiga

After the International Union for Conservation of Nature classified species as "critically endangered"

Is it a mystery ungulate illness
or exploding chemicals from Russian test rockets?
No one knows. I look for you in the space
between the window screen and eternity.
So many particles I cannot name them
yet they add up to fusion. Oh Saiga, you
and your bizarre bulging eyes roam the
Kazakhstan tundra. Why are you dying?
Is it something in the water? No human
rides your back – maybe you long to feel weight.
You have tired from frequenting the same
sand dunes, your spongy proboscis filtering out
dust. Your horns spiral out of control.
There is no need to butcher you anymore
for eastern fertility rituals, pocket the horns,
leave the carcass to rot. Man exploded
while you imploded. You do not know how to
communicate to the herd: *the worst predator.*

1-800-ART

magenta plastic frame
black and white Brooklyn Bridge

repurposed blue wooden frame
bemused Audrey Hepburn

blue and white striped frame
Mr. Met smiles

green with gold flecks
Wolf pack roaming nature scape

fire engine red rectangle
Mojave desert at night

thin wispy black metal frame
Picasso's three eyed woman glares

at us from every angle
dreams of looking straight ahead

Atypical Lines Heard on a First Date, or Wedge Wood Bear

Instead of((*I don't like to have to read at the movies))*
My palms will caress you like newly poured concrete, soft,
and everywhere at once, then hard, right at the end.

Instead of: ((*I climbed the highest totem on vacation))*
Don't be dry and earthly squeezed. Embody liquid silver.

Instead of: ((*I don't want to be your friend*))
I flew off the roof, shattered the sky,
broke the sun when I picked up your glasses.

Instead of: ((*So many things…mapquest))*
There was dirt under my finger nails in Texas.

Instead of: ((*I was in Germany for twenty minutes*))
I want to be a rhyming, white laced girl in the best horror film.

Instead of: ((*thread count is overrated))*
Shatter the wedge wood bear.
Black and blue is the new black.

Fertility Ritual at the 29th Parallel

Ultraviolet light judged my mistakes—
Oil sealed my third eye
shut.

Hands and feet, confiscated,
cooked,
left for later.

The casket waited
for rebirth
Shoulder blades twitched for

lack of wings.
Subsumed underground,
The crow's call, unanswered.

Shovel: the last precious tool.
Dig for a dark, sickening melted
thing.

Lavender and sage burned
I was reborn but subordinated
into slices of cake:

profiterole breasts,
pelvic flan
lady finger feet.

The crone's hands
caressed my abdomen
sensing too little activity?

Like she was trying
to get something going,
stoke the fire.

I knew she was a solid gold
spirit hunter, a convicted hag chaser
I was a giant piece of hippie candy.

Your lips will taste like hibiscus berry,
And chocolate will leak out of your pussy.

She knew all things. My sex was to hear,
not listen to who comes.

sound of chromosomes

There is no continental drift to xx. Glacial voice elevates between top teeth and soft palate, swallow inbox groans. No matter how hard one tries to expel nomenclature, the minor keys linger in all-night gas stations. My lovely contagion, wifi, beep beep bops its way to a century of silent films. Bottomless lust shattered commercials in outer space. My xx cannot nail down a simple one minute sound bite. I will announce how symbolic this is. My xx is not listed in emoticons. Channel seven stole my cat who ate the wishbone and regurgitated into smart phones and protest signs. My xx is smarter than your online chat but too emotional to practice an off switch. Make a boom boom base –no bronze hat rat tat tats. No virtue. Its sound cloud carves up pavement and old fashioned pool halls. My xx knows no resignation, emanates rage the exact moment lips get caught in a zipper. My xx is the feeling of bombastedness – stand back, play back that base.

The Stuntwoman Considers Ending it All

She is an adrenaline junkie.
In her third eye,
dirtied angel wings jut from scapulae.
Flying is a mindset.
What a sick twist.

The hungover crew sets up over a cliff.
Craft service has a hard time
keeping the carbs un-moist.

The male bit players wear leather,
punch and flip all over themselves.
Then, ACTION!!

She runs and hurls herself with glee
Over the muscle made brigade, over the mountain,
into the water below.
Applause.

The shot goes so well this could've
been a snuff film.
Afterall, what is death if not a show.

She braces against the ocean, like electricity
the waves flip on and off
over and under.

A Death Metal dirge will be added in post.
Blueblack leaps to meet her in a swirl of
comic/tragic mask choreography.

Like a competent dance partner,
the waves holds her well.
the fish open their mouths in one last "O."

The seaweed slime parts like Crispin Glover's hair.
She imagines last memories:

Her boyfriend's smoky tongue.
Chinese take-out with Lorraine.
Dress shopping for opening night.

The white tent above and behind her,
the blackness down deep,
easy and forever.

They say brain waves freeze
at the exact moment of passing.

Conscious thought drifts away,
a parallel universe opens up to us all.

Or it's just gray matter synapse nonsense
devised from too much PBS watching.

The PA's are agog,
but also bored
they yearn for violence.

And what is the ocean if not even keeled?

She's not dead, just plays it that way.
likes floating "in between" for a while,

feels her black eyeliner run down pancake makeup
away from her tough, chewed up soul.

The water is an eraser.
She will live to die again tomorrow.

Solstice

Cyclical:
forget how
to swallow,
fingertips
bluon particles
exiting a
cavernous
orifice
Incandescence:
electromagnetic sugar diversified
into mason jars
Nuclear fizzle:
heating pad
tendons on
what mystifies all physicians—
the lower back spines stupefy
Explosive:
Extracted teeth
found in the cellar
Invoke:
enkindled
doll skin
Revel:
mums scald
the world
an ignited
receiving
blanket
Calcify:
drought
damaged

roots and toes
Steel: an
aluminum
encased
body
sweltering
palms,
like
early onset
            dementia
Char : memory,
remains burned , scattered ash
My body:
            exists to
harden,
Brain waves:
            emblaze
planets
waiting for the burn
I didn't know I wanted

A Sparrow's Death

its own pecking mechanism frozen
black eyes gaze into a blue sky

void the star of the day is
already dead thousands of light

years away barreling toward a third eye
blistering against a sidewalk spine

how many kinds of light can I describe?
blinding, refractory, gentle but is

light ever gentle? the light is a
sniper not a tunnel beckoning from

the other side I greet the new day
aren't you a handsome devil hunting

moths in the dark who disappear,
needing the light but also tempting

suicide no you are dead already I
whisper into your moth wing

the black circular eye unblinking
ready to confront predators, even

if it is me, confronting my moth
strength for wing to wing to

spread to fly to land to evolve we
decide no, you do not evolve today

you must work for it

Backyard Poem #1

I paid too much for the color green, suffered through imitation Kermit voices or bacterial infections? Brown roots stay brown in chia pet grass planters. Your epidermis landscape is a close talker. The lawn gives foot massages after dinner but twigs are like a gangster's shiv -- hard as Legos under toes. Peace should just exist. So many Oms, netty pot cleanses, relaxation stations. Ladybugs are one winged angels flying in circles around Chai tea. Dandelion fuzz blows into future Folgers Coffee commercials from the 90s. Barrier reef sky is not a barrier if your I-pad falls out the window. Birthed through a sink hole, out pops Neil Degrasse Tyson and explains it all. Rabbits know the best edible flowers, their little rabbit fangs massacre the pansies.

Bird Poem #3

I dropped him off at the train station.
He sat amongst goldfish crumbs.
He drank an energy drink.
Only berries for breakfast
like the chipmunk
I saw run through the flower bed,
costumed in the structure of a man.
I dropped him off on the sidewalk.
He lugged a backpack.
The wind blew.
The rain poured.
Why don't you eat anymore?
I couldn't ask.
I wanted a smile and a "*next time…*"
I dropped him off at the train station.

Backyard Poem #8

The shiny green bottle flies swarm in the corner of the cherry tree. Like business men wearing the same suit from Men's Warehouse they buzz about looking for discounts. Bugs avoiding the swatter, no searching Google maps, movie ticket apps, no arguing over the cleanest stout. Following commercial flight paths they continually commute. Sniff out moist compost. Land, regurgitate, rub their legs together. They don't even know the species we named them: *Calliphoridae*. Survive, flourish. A robin plucks one by the back stairs and swallows it whole. The mob continues their busy work, eats, mates, return, repeat. The Fly nailed it. It's just too hard to mesh concepts. As the body changes the brain cannot handle it. In mostly fly body, Jeff Goldblum says he is "getting better." Don't sweat it Jeff, you look good with compound eyes and mouthparts.

She came out from under the bed #6

The wind-up toys all mismatched polarity and swapped

pull-string cacophony. The sun rose in the west today. Her tongue

squiggled and lashed, a hummingbird readied alpha state.

She dropped many seeds that day.

None so light as my trust and distrust.

She came out from under the bed #7

the others played it star struck.
Some got low, tried to obtain her autograph in secret,
tied her wrists together, sacked her head.
her tiny chicken scratch lines
engraved into the wood floor
some crouched behind chairs, kept lookout for hope
others in shock, fork in midair,
grasping handfuls of twigs and hair.
sucking the flies in

She came out from under the bed #8

the insects and fog

pushing from inside her abdomen,
skittered across diaphragm.
The *patpatpat*

she transferred to me.
hear the wasps
she mouthed a buzzing sound.

It wouldn't stop.
Will never stop.

This trying to get out.

She came out from under the bed #9

and I gave her what she wanted.
Let her in under the covers
she took my cavity warmth
my pummeled heart
my dueling catalyst brain waves
my wrapped limbs, protected thoughts
as the sand is smothered by salt
I was constricted in dark
dust, the bones of my childhood,
crying out to turn on the light.

Someone was coming up the stairs.

Dear J #1

The sky broke.
Sunset became a fatality in
my train-track
backyard.

Maples blazed up,
giant persimmons against
the battleship sky.
This time of year,

trees in the Midwest are
on fire with color.
Clouds: ash and smoke.
I've got itchy feet.

There are new faces.
Not as many Nick Cave
fans to bring me my Jam Jar drinks.
I like to be served with pretension.

Have you reaped vineyards?
Hid from helicopters?
Where is your center?
I am a ventriloquist's dummy.

Dear M #2

Vineyard vines choke me.
My horde costume split.
Manikins are jealous.
They wish they could split

down the center but
plastic is impossible
to slice with impoliteness.

New guts weld together
by The Silver Spider.
Pumpkin lattes rust
all tourist faces.

Rattling in my plastic
PVC pipe skull
is a Bad Finger impression.
Before lip gloss,

before conspicuous consumption,
I could buy my pipe anywhere.
What do you play at game night?
O Brother Where Art Thou?

Knee socks are Kroger's.
Nurse is the new cleaners.
Only candy is sold
at the nail salon.

We have become too bright.
We eat muted calcium deposits.
How non-Buddhist.
Every bumper sticker, my face.

Dear J #3

Lose yourself in the woods.
I place trinkets
in tree-hollows for squirrels to find.
They are not edible.

I don't venture out of county.
Here is the place to live
in case of a zombie uprising.
You can see anything coming.

I pick them off from tree-tops.
I don't like to play games
that have too many rules.
Stick to UNO.

If we're talking nostalgia,
then I miss Pepsi-Free
from glass bottles.
My grandparents had those in their basement.

It tasted like medicine,
but also comfort.
This time of year
is cheese curds and hard sausage logs.

I guess that's why so many people have summer birthdays.
What is dangerous where you are?
Parents give their kids names
like window cleaner.

I'll laugh when the salt
starts eating up the roads.

Dear M #5

The ghost dreamt
a pox on our new house.

She turns on the bedroom
light at 4:30 am
It is not faulty wiring.

Dead static wanders through colonial
walls like vandalized smoke,
explodes into mail box forget-me-nots.

I hear a girl crying
when I am alone in bed.
When I open the door to the hallway,
the crying stops like
yanking on a parking break.

Her sadness locked in a safe.
I expect to hear crying
nightly now
so it is a moot issue.

A stomach growl would be
louder than my apathy
and gain more attention.
I am envious of my own track,

this yearning in the gut,
churning muscle,
looking for nutrients
to hold.

To hold
and then relinquish all bits
and chewed up pieces,
absolve itself of responsibility.

Dear J #6

Phantoms covet modern conveniences.
Electricity is a wonder.
Pipes; a dream.
If your lights are flickering,

it's just curiosity.
Outside, rose bushes
Are hacked to thorns,
your ghost will
prefer a fireplace

to central heating.
Apparitions claw dry wall.
I just roll over.
My bone marrow

is full of frost
I feel scattered,
dwelling with crazies.
Who knows best

how to play bad cop/good cop?
It's the live ones who
fret all day and
eat toaster pastries.

The old ones crow:
eat more,
sleep more,
eat more,
sleep more.

We wake every day to tourniquets and maimed limbs.

Backyard Poem #12

On Tuesdays and Thursdays it was off to the dinosaur lady's house. An albino dinosaur who always wore velour, she liked sugar puffs. I rough housed with her little dinosaur offspring. The offspring was names Eric. I played the part of the caveman. He would slam into me and punch me in the sides and gut. The elementary school was just a ten minute walk through a dirt path in the woods behind their lair. *I'll chase you through the woods, if you get to school first, I won't throw you over my shoulder, skin you like a potato.* One day I threw my elbow up into his teeth. Both of us spilled our prehistoric dinosaur blood. At ten, I masked my fire breath walking into home room, my razor-like claws raked the wood desk.

.

vultures 1

a child flaps

under a swimming pool tarp

pop shake point spray

cut 409 poison

a dragging

top of a flat-bed truck

lay in the field,

left for possessive bear scat

A raw piece of metal

scraped against the earth's skin

I watched

generator cranking,

gearing up to slam

They sun themselves

wings spread, don't you know?

shade like gunshots

(no vultures)

history text book or bruised apple

can of beer or MRSA virus

hair net against the apex of humanity

dead bolt lock blocks a lost tool belt

A quickening before a steady heart beat

surgical steel or malignant tumor

wounded crane or jagged window

repurposed paper or saltwater inlet

mouse or muffler

bag of sweet tarts or melted question

a paper doll or wind up doorbell chronicle

Prague mission after New York bodega

a pen vandalizes a notebook

because more doing than done too

Bird Poem #4

Ticks removed: two
No, three
one discovered the next day
on a hip

bluebells un-bloomed all week
Leafy, convoluted brain stems
Muck splattered shoes
Stomped hay grass

Blue birds never showed
Empty little wood boxes
Listen for the call
Muster up a sh sh sh sh sh

Sounds like *she she she*
Come to me me me
How successful was my bird call?
Blue birds almost went extinct in VA

The dominant sparrows
cleared out the nests
Bird bullies
Some humans trapped and killed the sparrows

Doesn't that make them a bully?
No, murderer.
I want something perched on my shoulder
Then I will be satisfied

Untouchable, like a memory
You never will of course

Just a hint of turquoise in the forest
Always struggling to build a home

Always the renter
Me, deluded

vultures II

I do not know the name for wing tipped flattery but I understand the need for flight

carnivorous bird is too big for any right wing living

ignites chest paralysis

I am a trail of silence

the only bird call I know is *indignant scream*

prey is fidgety marmoset

talons rake the pillow

It's not nevermore, never was, this raven tattooed on my back

stays away

the beak won't stop popping all my thought bubbles

Diviner

I met a witch while
getting the mail
eyes black as frostbite
tentacle hair static clinging
all over make believe.
Non Madrigal tones, she
expelled chalk dust,
gesticulated a
hang man's game,
her blades, sharp.
You haven't bent your back
far enough to witness
a tree canopy
on the ground,
sky in pay dirt.
She measured my forearms,
pummeled my muscles with theory
With forked tongue she healed
river beds, now my veins,
sucked minerals dry,
my wasted words,
a sunny day.
You hack
waste machine
what new hells bells are these?
To answer, she
spread my fingers wide,
eyelashes wider
ciphered a message buried
beneath my breastbone.
Her incantation:
suffocate the quiet.

My arms banked,
destined for shaman gold,
sounds in my skull reverberated
against flickering stops.
She flourished:
open your throat.

hotel movie

one hotel
room unlocked
door pushes
open a red
door from
the outside
(green from
the inside)
snowy
T.V.
owl
perched on
a towel
rack
blinking
message light
bobcat tears
up the sheets
not a woman,
an actual bobcat
white swans
decimate the
bible by beak
don't you see?
violent
swans
challenge
stereotypes

real doors

wood
faux
metal
sliding glass
particle board
dormitory
motel 6
Special 8
Best Western
Holiday Inn
Holiday Express
Two way
Three way
Four way
townhouse
apartment
suburban ranch
suburban colonial
Invisible
fictional
hanging
Apollo 13
storm
French
Spanish
Byzantium
_____ man
antique barn
repurposed
dollhouse
miniature
fairy

Elven
Smurf
zoo
front
back
rotating
trap
trick
adult movie:
The Green _____
poorly lit
neon bar
dungeon
garage
Isa____a Duncan
outhouse
open
ajar
closed
hermetically sealed

hotel movie 2

It always starts with a horse in the room,
watching a horse on T.V. a deer walks into a bar,
sees it's antlers on the wall—too late.

Alma Hale, you Flightless Bird

After 'Bowl of Irises, by Alma Hale, early twentieth century.

I will not be here tomorrow afternoon to gaze upon you. Another determined tourist will gaze upon you or ignore you to write at this massive writing desk. Though we are forced to look at you. The windows placed too high, near the roof, too high to catch a glimmer of sunshine. The garden a mix of fallen stone heads with cracked noses, the Black eyed Susans, sunken , the fire pit damp. All we have is the painting of irises.

Alma, you must be dead now, with a name like Alma. I cannot bear to think about those irises in a bowl, so carefully assembled at the time, the correct color for the bowl chosen with precision before lunch, the arc of the flowers sketched ahead of time. Should they be cut at an angle or lay loose? The water level barely noticeable, as fitting for water levels.

Alma did you know what brush you would begin with? Thick horse hair bristles? A delicate etching tool? Did you plan to smother the canvas in all one color, before layer upon layer smoothed out all of those rough edges? Did you delight in those tiny mistakes? Did you move onto a slim brush, to detail the yellow centers of the flowers? How much time did you have to paint? To catch the afternoon light just right before visitors entered the house, created a ruckus? Did your work go unglorified while you put dinner on the stove or laced up boots to muck out the stable?

Alma I know you were a whole human, Did you experience enough or were the irises a symbol of your quietness? How far did your eyes travel Alma? Your irises landed here, in this artist's colony bedroom in Virginia. A golden lab lay on the carpet at night. There is a huge library of books downstairs with a sign that says, *thieves welcome.*

In the end it is a just a vapid bowl of flowers that fades into wall paper. Maybe you 've got the right idea. Sitting there, on the wall. We act like we are so present in the world, but you have nowhere else to go, nowhere else to be.

You wait.

Until the owners move or die, you stay there. Maybe that is truly the way to judge ourselves. When all around us is movement: be still.

Backyard Poem #13

Marc outside. "Is the 'c' pretentious?" my friend Meg asked. The blanket perpendicularly sweaty to us because his muscles were too big. My dress too short. But it was dark. Marc said no one could see us. His hands started to move. It was as if *that* shone the spotlight on. Twinkly porch lights gleamed from the backyard like Friday Night Lights. LED garden posts flickered with paranormal activity. Red Chinese lanterns glowed in cherry blossoms. Mid sedan headlights swiveled around the cul-de-sac like popcorn bulbs from a carousel. Watches pulsed with little alien eyes. The neighbors' pool reflected a Carnival Cruise. Police crime scene. Times Square. The fucking full moon. It didn't happen for us that night, outside at a friend's BBQ when everyone else was wearing cashmere, stirring another mixed drink, discussing my youth in their well-lit upstate home. I remember Marc said, *you're wet just because of the humidity.*

Bird poem #5

overly cheerful marigolds
confront four furry feet

tread lightly on the mulch,
black seeds, crab grass

warmth is for swallowing not plowing
you have no hands to fight him off

what will become of the beak?
the brain? the gossamer brownness

our barely there flight paths

Every Her Dies

(Eyes)

We weren't aware of them at first. The first silhouette a place holder wedged in between the pines. Decayed matter is easier to squish. August dusk, always uncertain. Junebug, Aunt Margaret, and I sat in that rambler with wood paneled walls on the back screened porch. I saw laser beam eyes peering through the wire fence squares. Aunt Margaret crocheted a toilet paper holder that looked like a doll's salsa skirt. Junebug read Historical fiction. I wasn't surprised by the visitor. Hostas were their favorite treat. Not wanting to leave. Or look away. I pretended to look through People.

A summons: mammal, predator, remains.

(After Aunt Margaret Built a Higher Fence)

When the motion detector light lit up we knew they lost their fear of humans. Days earlier they opened their mouths and gnawed on the azaleas over the nylon mesh fence that now sat on top of the four foot metal one. Now blue tongues were all that lay in between their teeth. Palate ulcers, damaged pharynx, eroded esophagus, forced anorexia. All things in pain do not cry out. The light flickered. When four legs come for you, you want to be different, you want a gun. They just wanted erasing. Or maybe it was us. Nudging heads into fence holes, bleeding. We ate cold soup for dinner. We tried to ignore the nudgings.
Tonight it is four.

An invocation: go away go away go away.

(Nurse)

I dreamt I put my palm on its flank. The fur was soft and still intact. The skin taunt, a feeling of wildness. But lumps moved under the pelt. Against my better judgment, my sleeping face lowered and nuzzled the mass, tried to flatten the lumps. A human iron, pounding away at infection with my cheeks and lips. Trying to comfort and save comfort and save comfort. The lumps, restless. They burst. The hoard released, seeking a new home. Ready for a second go round? I woke. Aunt Margaret baked a meat pie with leftovers. We trim the tree and sweep hard surfaces. We complete quiet activities.

One discourse: do not sleep.

(Early)

Some people are brave in daylight. Men drive around in trucks calling in reports. Junebug, Aunt Margaret, and I return from the store to see a doe lying down in a shallow pool of dirty water. My thoughts become those of a text book: Deer lay in water to reduce the blood boiling fever. With damaged hooves, some deer can be found crawling on chests or knees.
They did not disappear into the woods that night. Swollen heads reached in through fence holes. One had already a caught a string of holiday lights around its engorged neck: a reminder of time and place. Another salivated noticeably. Gleaming spider webs of poison filled spit- diamonds. Junebug made a rushed dinner as if we had somewhere to be. We hadn't. Junebug muttered, "It is their burden." Then why are we afraid.

A sound: A bleating.

(What We Hear)

outbreak of Epizootic Hemorrhagic Disease has been ongoing STOP white-tailed

STATIC deer Illinois, (beat) Indiana, (beat) Michigan, (beat)

some cases were reported in Iowa breath Drought conditions increase breath make it worse

Deer congregate for water biting midge and that is. STOP (Culicoides

variipennis) and that is. and the disease thrive. the

hundreds of deer have died *what did he.*

Fish, Wildlife, and Parks biologists drag carcasses out of the Clark Fork River more beating.

If you find an ill or dead deer, call 1-800-356-5680 and tell them where it is, wait. give the coordinates get a pencil of the ill or dead deer,

what the sex is, when it was found, where

was it? what it yes? looks like.

The News says that Medications are given to cattle to cure them from EHD.

The News use phrases like STOP brow line, wide as ears, dark at the base, and velvet. Put this in the pot.

Fact: It doesn't affect the taste of the meat.

(Others)

Skin sloughs off. The sloughing is the second movement. Rapid pulse rate is the concerto. Maybe the white ghost appears as a special guest. Interruption of pieces, of cell growth. Hooves break. In extreme cases the deer die within 8-36 hours. The worst is the blood. Hemorrhaging of the skin. The most visible of the inside coming out. Bonds and ligaments bursting apart. Upper lips curl up, in madness. Cell walls in the heart, lungs, and diaphragm weaken and burst. Deer infected with the an acute form pass into a shock-like state, become prostrate, and then die.

They don't act like themselves. We don't like ourselves.
Warren county: Quarantined.

A Footnote: Cosmopolitan states that asking for help is sometimes the hardest thing of all.

(She didn't mean for it to happen this way)

Junebug plays the organ in the living room. Music accomplishes what speaking does not: breaking through to the other side. Circle the organ three times. Avoid the upper register. Raise your left arm and put your backhand on forehead. This mimics the distress pose. Help pamphlets will then be distributed to car windshields.

The wall faces smile down at Junebug as she plays: such clean hair parts. If you always part your hair in the same place, it is said to grow wider; hair reaching to make its own end, its own piece of business. Pieces of some things are dying in the backyard. We join human and animal in the second measure. Junebug's relatives in Canada do not call. She sings of heat and hearts, throws her voice against the walls. It is a lifting. Afterwards, a scavenger hunt in the yard for parts. Afterwards, illegal burials. We all deserve to wear white.

A favorite line from the song: I know where the bodies are.

(Affects)

I sit at Junebug's vanity and brush my long brown hair. I look down at the wood table next to me where there is a painting. It's a still life of a picnic spread in the hills of Parma. Olive trees surround a feast. I feel the warmth of the sun- not blinding hot, light, like a lemon drop. Delicate. A comforting cliché. Then thick black paint floods the spring watercolor I just created minutes earlier. I did not spill the paint. I don't know where it is coming from. It looks like oil. It smothers the airy colors of turquoise, canary yellow, rose, green apple. I cannot move to stop it. I cannot stop the pollution. I cannot breathe. My hair wrapped around my neck. My head on the wall.

Beauty tip: Under my hair is fur.

(The Cast)

Place: The Midwest.

The Ranch: old paint, some wood paneling, photos of grandkids on the walls, needs updated plumbing, some flowered wall paper. Clean.

Garden: Spacious, contains many flowering plants, gnomes, gourd birdhouses, has blood in it.

Me: a girl, Alive.

Junebug: A grandmother figure. Likes to garden, A matriarch, Alive.

Aunt Margaret (Junebug's step-daughter, girl's Aunt): Cooks, works at a car repair place, Alive.

Deer: infected, dead.

(The Frost)

The cycle is anywhere from five to ten years. The biting midge is the vector. Lovely pools evolve into livid viral slops of bug infestation. Year six is biting and mixing. Year seven is swirling blood chew fur fat. Year eight is repetitious dripping. Year nine is swollen swallows of eggs. Year ten is bursting and inflammation bite spot death. Year future is stomping ground shooter stinger mite teeth plunge poison sickness that hops from warmth to warmth to warmth and finally explodes and hunters drag another carcass out of the lake. Year eternity is at your door step.

Temperature: Frigid.

(Protein)

Ranchers medicate the herd if the cattle become infected. The cattle don't graze as much due to mouth and throat pain, and this affects their weight/ meat. Pick up a bottle Banamine Injectable Solution at Valley Vet. Load up on Dexamethasone. Afterwards put wild flowers in the jars to make a pretty table center piece.

Hooves become lame. Wear black patent leather heels to create empathy. Offer Flunixamine in the soft palm of your hand. They will lick it up straight away.
Other than that, cattle ranchers are not affected.

Midges breed in one hoof print puddle or slime covered tree bark. The females require blood for their eggs to mature.

The females bloodfeed at dawn or dusk. Thrust, parry, thrust. She won't taste the meds.

(Rack)

Objects become different when you remember their owner. The brown tracks of the past hardened knobs along the base, tiny threads of fibrous life at the cut-off point. A few strands of fur remain. Something seen before but now on the ground and glistening. The smoothest and hardest thing ever made of animal and mineral at the same time. A game of pick up Stix.

Made to battle, to crush, to prove. Interlaced in between my fingers, give me some hardness, some stones to kill. Let me remain unburied, unburned.

Collect: End of summer antler mineralization gets hard fast. Sheds velvet. A velvet purse with a woodsy theme.

Shelve.

Then, like dryer lint, discard. It'll wash up.

(Fibers)

Come home come home I heard from in the bath. Then I hear gun shots. Hoof and tooth, nail and antler, hair and smile, eyes and small ears. Fibers. Threads. Various elongated cells of sinewy structures. My fibers can be stretched. Cotton fibers can be woven into yarn. My bones can break into rocks. I can use antlers as bones in my wrists and ankles. In summer the antlers grow ¼ inch a day. These materials can be Fiber'd into my being. They can promote intestinal slough-age once inside.

My own vocal chords, bleating. The long strips of tough tissue breaking out and open. Dries on a slab. Cured. Now nothing can get in. A delicacy.

I decay so slowly it is a joke. Not meant for time. Focus through my force. My fuse.

My palatial wounds split in the woods.

(Present)

An anomaly, with red eyes and white fur, tourists camped out overnight in Solon, Iowa just to capture a photograph of this elusive candy-eyed, beige hooved, white ghost. Native Americans believed the white deer were spiritual messengers and possessed healing powers. A walking trauma center, the albino deer is such a rarity- only one in every 100,000 deer. Poor eye sight and because it does not blend within its surroundings, things eat it.

I am docile, giving. I lay in the grass for you, so many legs, magic on the ground now at your fingertips. I draw you to me like a minx covered in sweet clover. I will pet you and say there…there.

My eyes are warm and pink and see through you, see through your meat. You yeast filled creature from the netherworld forest of grime and insects.

Not immune to the midge monster, I celebrate your carcass by putting a bow in it.

(The Beginning)

A plate of warm chocolate chip oatmeal cookies sits on the outdoor picnic table. Aunt Margaret and Junebug clink short whiskey-filled glasses. It is a humid July day in Michigan. The rose bushes are five feet tall and the magenta Azaleas taller. The emperor Hostas are a force. I have to stand on my tip toes to water the tallest flowering plants. Junebug instructs me to water more than I think it needs it. "What they don't eat in mine, they devour in others," Junebug says, almost offended.

We go inside.

The deer, post-card perfect and full of Bambi jump over the four foot metal fence, as graceful as can be.

(Tidings)

I turn the handle of the screen door, peek outside. Little brown hotels crash and float down dirty rivers. Fixed shapes come apart quickly and slowly.

The mingling hum of electricity and wire: body and forest. Home and hearth, earth only a few feet deep. The core was closer than we thought.

Magic welded the walls together: hovers between brain, center, air. Bones still hard- check. We do not say yes, we do not use affirmations.

We rely on a Field and Stream. Elements grouped into oxygen, chords, carbon, tar, calcium, teeth, hydrogen, excrement, grease calls for a soap bucket.

Observe decay chains and reactions.

It is Winter.

Acknowledgements

Some of these poems first appeared in the following journals, sometimes slightly altered:

Moss Trill, *e*ratio*, *Gargoyle*, *The Infoxicated Corner*, *The Offbeat*, *The Norfolk Review*, *Rogue Agent*, *So to Speak*, *Kind of a Hurricane Press: Storm Cycle Anthology*, *Really System*, *The Northern Virginia Review*, *Pretty Owl Poetry*, *Red Savina Review*, *Toad Suck Review*, *Uut Poetry*, *Thirteen Myna Birds*, *Inferior Planets*, *F.A.L.D.*, *Degenerate Lit*, *Hermeneutic Chaos*, *Three Drops from the Cauldron Anthology*, *Queen Mob's Teahouse*, *In the Words of Womyn 2016 International Anthology*, *The Opiate Magazine*, *Sweet Tree Review*, *Sea Foam Magazine*, *Lime Hawk*, *Birds: A Flight of Poems Anthology* by Feral Press, and *Hobart Pulp*.

"The Hour" and "The Stuntwoman Considers…" were also published in the chapbook *Clown Machine* (Grey Book Press, 2016.)

"a sparrow's death" was nominated for a Pushcart Prize by *Northern Virginia Review.*

The chapbook, *Every Her Dies* was first published by ELJ Publications, 2014 and published online at the Poetry Center Chapbook Exchange in 2017.

Included "Backyard Poems" were collected in a chapbook published by Dancing Girl Press, 2015.

"Dear M" and "Dear J" poems were co-written with Meg Tisinger.

Notes

Epizootic hemorrhagic disease (EHD) is a hemorrhagic disease of white-tailed deer (Odocoileus virginianus) caused by an infection of a virus from the genus Orbivirus. It is an infectious, and sometimes fatal, virus that is characterized by extensive hemorrhages, and is found throughout the United States.

Some EHD information taken from the Michigan Department of Natural Resources:

About the Author

Jennifer MacBain-Stephens lives in the Midwest and is the author of three full-length poetry collections: *Your Best Asset is a White Lace Dress* (Yellow Chair Press 2016), *The Messenger is Already Dead* (Stalking Horse Press 2017), and *The Vitamix and the Murder of Crows*, recently out from Apocalypse Party. Her work has been nominated for Best of the Net and the Pushcart Prize. She is also the author of ten chapbooks. Recent work can be seen at or is forthcoming from *The Pinch*, *Black Lawrence Press*, *Quiddity*, *Prelude*, *Cleaver*, *Yalobusha Review*, d*ecomp*, and *Inter/rupture*.

Visit: http://jennifermacbainstephens.wordpress.com

About this Book

We're Going to Need a Higher Fence contains poems that were inspired by a line in Robert Frost's piece "Mending Wall:" "Before I built a wall I'd ask to know what I was walling in or walling out." It would seem that we look to nature for some kind of healing or finding answers to life's problems, but often our surroundings provide more questions, no peace, and even unexpected violence. Instead of walling out the "bad things," that seem to find a way in anyway, maybe the answer is to try and exist side by side with these dark shadows. There is no escaping the unknown, disease, pain, etc: these are things we will never have control over. I struggle to find acceptance of this concept, but maybe struggle is okay.

www.ingramcontent.com/pod-product-compliance
Lightning Source LLC
Chambersburg PA
CBHW031208090426
42736CB00009B/825
9781943170296